LIVES
AND
TIMES

Harriet Tubman

John Rowley

**Heinemann Interactive Library,
Des Plaines, Illinois**

Published by Heinemann Interactive Library,
an imprint of Reed Educational & Professional Publishing,
1350 East Touhy Avenue, Suite 240 West
Des Plaines, IL 60018

Produced by Times Offset (M) Sdn. Bhd.
Designed by Ken Vail Graphic Design.
Illustrations by Sean Victory

02 01 00 99 98
10 9 8 7 6 5 4 3 2 1

Library of Congress Cataloging-in-Publication Data

Rowley, John, 1955–
    Harriet Tubman/John Rowley,
        p. cm. -- (Lives and times)
    Includes bibliographical references and index.
    Summary: A simple biography of the woman who escaped life as a slave and then rescued other slaves as a conductor in the Underground Railroad.
    ISBN 1-57572-558-4 (lib. bdg.)
    1. Tubman, Harriet, 1820?–1913 -- Juvenile literature. 2. Slaves -- United States -- Biography -- Juvenile literature. 3. Afro-Americans -- Biography -- Juvenile literature. 4. Afro-American women -- Biography -- Juvenile literature. (1. Tubman, Harriet, 1820?–1913. 2. Slaves. 3. Afro-Americans -- Biography. 4. Women -- Biography.) I. Title. II. Series: Lives and times (Crystal Lake, Il1.)
E444.T82R69 1997
973'.0496073'0092 -- dc21
[B]   97-13730
                                                            CIP
                                                            AC

Some words are shown in bold, **like this**. You can find out what they mean by looking in the glossary. The glossary also helps you say difficult words.

Acknowledgments
The author and publishers are grateful to the following for permission to reproduce copyright photographs:
Chris Honeywell, p. 21; Hulton Deutsch, pp. 18–19;
Schlesinger Library, Radcliffe College, p. 22; Sophia Smith Collection, pp. 16–17.

Cover photograph: Sophia Smith Collection

Special thanks to Betty Root for her comments in the preparation of this book.

Every effort has been made to contact copyright holders of any material reproduced in this book. Any omissions will be rectified in subsequent printings if notice is given to the publisher.

Contents

Part One

This is the story of a very special person named Harriet Tubman. Harriet was a real woman. This is a true story.

Harriet was born in the state of Maryland in 1821, about 180 years ago. Harriet's grandparents were born in Africa.

Harriet's family lived on a **plantation**. She had ten brothers and sisters. They all had to work for the man who owned the plantation.

Harriet and her family were **slaves**. This meant that they were not allowed to leave the plantation and they had to do exactly what they were told.

When Harriet was six, she had to start work. She never went to school. She worked all day in the fields. Harriet was always very tired.

The **plantation** owner was very cruel. He
hit the **slaves** to make them work harder.
Once, Harriet tried to stop him from
hitting someone. He cracked her **skull**.

When Harriet was 28 years old, she ran away. She went to a state where people did not have **slaves**.

She found a job in a hotel, but she was not
happy. Harriet kept thinking about her family.
She decided to go back to rescue them.

It was very dangerous for Harriet to go back to the **plantation**. She had to **disguise** herself so no one would know that she was an escaped **slave**. She was very brave.

Harriet made 19 journeys. She **smuggled** 300 slaves out of Maryland. She moved them through a network of secret, safe hiding places. This network was known as the **Underground Railroad**.

During the Civil War (1861–1865), Harriet helped the Union side, which was fighting to free the **slaves**. First, she became a **spy**. Then she became a nurse.

When Harriet was old, she helped look
after some of the people she had rescued.
They all lived together in a big house.

Part Two

We know that Harriet Tubman was a real person. This is a photograph of her with some of the people she helped. She is the woman on the left of the photograph.

There are no photographs of Harriet as a young girl. We have to imagine what she looked like.

This is a photograph of a **plantation**. The plantation that Harriet lived on when she was young was like this. Looking at it helps us see what her life was like.

You can see the **slaves** working in the field and the guard watching over them. This picture shows us how hard the work was.

Harriet never learned to read or write, because she never went to school. When Harriet was an old lady, she told her story to her friend, Sarah Bradford.
Sarah wrote down Harriet's story for her. This is a page from that book. The book tells us all about Harriet's life.

HARRIET TUBMAN.

Harriet Tubman

THE MOSES OF HER PEOPLE

by Sarah Bradford

Introduction by Butler A. Jones

THE CITADEL PRESS
Secaucus, New Jersey

Harriet was 93 when she died. She was a very important person in the fight against slavery. People wanted to remember her.

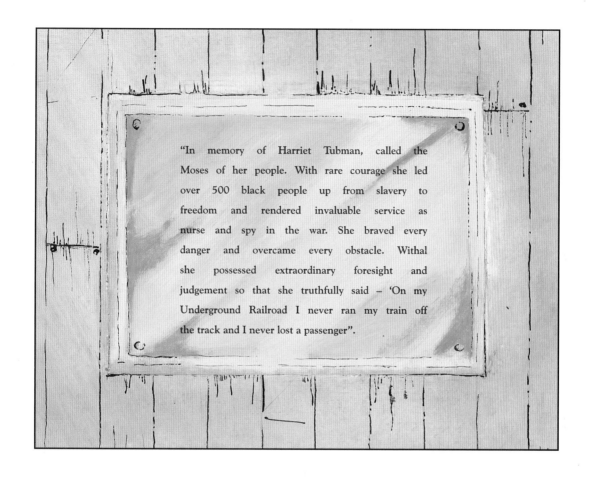

"In memory of Harriet Tubman, called the Moses of her people. With rare courage she led over 500 black people up from slavery to freedom and rendered invaluable service as nurse and spy in the war. She braved every danger and overcame every obstacle. Withal she possessed extraordinary foresight and judgement so that she truthfully said – 'On my Underground Railroad I never ran my train off the track and I never lost a passenger".

Some of the people she had helped decided to make a special sign. They put it on her house. They did not want the story of Harriet Tubman ever to be forgotten.

Glossary

This glossary explains difficult words, and helps you to say words which may be hard to say.

disguise Dressing up so people do not know who you are. You say *dis GIZE.*

plantation This is a large farm where the workers live on the farm. You say *plan TAY shun.*

skull Bones in your head form your skull.

slave Person who is forced to work for another person and is never free. Slaves are owned, and can be bought and sold.

smuggling Secretly moving things, or people, from one place to another.

spy Person who finds out secrets.

Underground Railroad Network of secret places where escaping slaves hid. It was not a real railroad, but the hiding places were called stations and the routes between them lines.

Index

More Books to Read

Adler, David. *A Picture Book of Harriet Tubman.* New York: Holiday, 1992

McLoone, Margo. *Harriet Tubman.* Mankato, Minn: Capstone Press, 1997